Reading Worksh

Reading Worksheets is a book of 44 photocopy masters designed for use with who are improving their reading skills.

Each page contains a short piece of everyday reading matter followed by questions and exercises which test the reader's understanding and develop reading skills. The book as a whole contains a wide variety of exercises but almost all the worksheets include a set of comprehension questions in a standard format *(True/False/Maybe* or *Yes/No/Don't know).* Increasing familiarity with these formats and the fact that many words and phrases are regularly repeated should make it easier for students to use the worksheets independently. The majority of the exercises require little writing or spelling skill and even those which do could be tackled orally.

The order in which the worksheets are arranged in the book should be regarded only as a very rough guide to their level of difficulty. The reader's individual interests and needs should dictate the suitability of a particular worksheet. Students with very limited reading ability should be able to attempt parts of many of the worksheets with the support of a tutor. An index *(p.48)* highlights some of the main topics covered in the worksheets.

No answers are given for the exercises because they can usually be found in the text itself. Sometimes the answer is open to debate and may depend on an ability to read between the lines or to apply personal knowledge of a topic. In a few cases, readers may need to refer to a standard reference book such as a dictionary, thesaurus or atlas.

Second edition

In this second edition, many of the worksheets have been revised and updated. Some sheets have been replaced and the titles of others have been changed. The order of contents has been rearranged, so this edition should not be used alongside the original one.

The material in **Reading Worksheets** *is suitable for use at Entry Level & Level 1 of the Adult Literacy Core Curriculum and the National Qualifications Framework.*

Please read the Copying & Reproduction restrictions below.

Publishers: Brown and Brown,
               Keeper's Cottage,
               Westward,
               Wigton
               Cumbria CA7 8NQ
               Tel. 016973 42915

First published 1993

Reprinted 1995, 1999, 2001 & 2004

Second edition 2006

ISBN   1 904874 09 6 *(10 digit)*
       978 1 904874 09 6 *(13 digit)*

Printed by Reed's Ltd., Penrith, Cumbria on 100% recycled paper and card.

Contents

Railway Station signs

A. True / False / Maybe

1. Platform 8 is down to the left.

2. Platform 5 is down to the right.

3. Information is down to the right.

4. The buffet is down to the left.

5. The way out is down to the right and left.

6. The toilets are down to the left.

7. The signs are on a bridge over the platforms.

8. Platforms 1, 2 and 3 are behind you.

B. Match the symbols to the words

Way out (right) **Toilets** **Buffet** **Taxis**

Platforms **Information** **Way out** (left)

a b c d e f g

Small ad.

> **FOR SALE** 3 ft bed, blue metal frame, with mattress, used only twice as guest bed, cost £180, sell for £60. Tel. 350319

A. True / False / Maybe

1. The bed is brand new.

2. The mattress is blue.

3. The frame is metal.

4. The sale price is £120 less than the cost price.

5. The bed has been used by 2 guests.

B. Fill in the missing words in these sentences

1. A 3 ft bed is ____ sale.

2. The bed has only been used ____.

3. The ____ cost £180 when new.

4. The bed has a mattress ____ a blue metal frame.

C. How many ?

1. How many words in the ad. begin with **f** ?

2. How many words in the ad. end in **e** ?

3. How many words in the ad. have **s** in them ?

4. How many numbers are there in the ad. ?

A note on the door

a.

> BT
> Key at N° 38 →

b.

> BT
> Key under mat

c.

> BT
> Back in 10 minutes

d.

> BT
> Had to go out.
> Come back tomorrow.

A. True / False / Maybe

1. BT is coming to mend the phone.
2. The person in the flat is out.
3. The door is locked.
4. All the notes could help a burglar.
5. No. 38 is to the right.

B. What do you think ?

1. Which notes let BT get into the flat at once ?
2. Which note means that BT will have to wait to get in ?
3. Which note means that BT will not get in today ?
4. Which note is the best one for a burglar to see ?
5. Which note shows that a neighbour is trusted ?
6. Which note, if any, would you leave on your door ?

Joke

Patient	I've got this very bad pain in my right arm, doctor.
Doctor	Don't worry, it's just old age.
Patient	Well, in that case, why doesn't my left arm hurt too ? I've had it just as long.

A. True / False / Maybe

1. The patient has a pain in his right arm.

2. The patient has a pain in his left arm.

3. The doctor doesn't think the pain is important.

4. The patient is an old woman.

5. The doctor is a young man.

B. Which word is missing ?

1. I've got this very pain in my right arm.

2. Why doesn't my arm hurt too ?

3. It's just old.

4. I've had it just long.

C. Write these out as two words

I've

Don't

It's

Doesn't

Tablets on Prescription

100 CO-CODAMOL EFFERVESCENT TABLETS
Two to be taken four times a day
MIX IN WATER FIRST BEFORE TAKING
MAXIMUM 2 TABLETS PER DOSE
MAXIMUM 8 TABLETS IN 24 HOURS

A. True / False / Maybe

1. Tablets must be mixed with water.

2. Four tablets to be taken two times a day.

3. Maximum 8 tablets per dose.

4. Maximum 8 tablets in a day.

B. Which word is missing ?

1. Two to be four times a day.

2. Maximum tablets in 24 hours.

3. Maximum 2 per dose.

4. Mix water first before taking.

C. Make the words in the box into one sentence

day	taken	times	tablets
two	to	four	a	be

Verse from a Greetings Card

Violets are red,
Roses are blue,
I'm colour blind
But I'm thinking of you!

A. Which word ?

1. Which words appear twice in the verse ?

2. Which words contain *in* ?

3. Which word contains the word *let* ?

4. Which word is short for 'I am' ?

5. Which 2 words rhyme in the verse ?

B. Join the 2 halves of the words

ro	our
think	lets
vio	ses
col	ing

C. Make up your own

Make up a verse of your own which begins:

Roses are red,
Violets are blue.......

Goldfish

the scene of the crime
was a goldfish bowl
goldfish were kept
in the bowl at the time

that was the scene
and that was the crime

Alan Jackson

A. Answer these questions

1. What was the crime ?

2. Where did it take place ?

3. Whodunnit ?

4. Which lines in the poem rhyme ?

5. Does the poem need punctuation and capital letters ?
   If so, where would you put them ?

B. Make up your own

Make up your own version of the poem by replacing the words *goldfish* and *bowl* with other words.

Hospital sign

Patients requiring Ambulance
Service Transport should
inform the Ambulance Liaison
Officer and then take
a seat in the waiting area.

A. True / False / Maybe

1. The hospital will transport patients by ambulance.

2. The Ambulance Liaison Officer is in the waiting area.

3. The waiting area has seats.

4. The Ambulance Liaison Officer will make you wait.

5. The Ambulance Liaison Officer is a man.

6. The waiting area is full of patients.

B. How many ?

1. How many words in the sign begin with a capital letter ?

2. How many words in the sign begin with **t** ?

3. How many words in the sign end with **e** ?

4. How many words in the sign have **an** in them ?

5. Which is the shortest word in the sign ?

6. Which are the longest words in the sign ?

C. Word meanings

Find a word in the sign which means the same as each of these:

tell   **needing**   **chair**

Street map

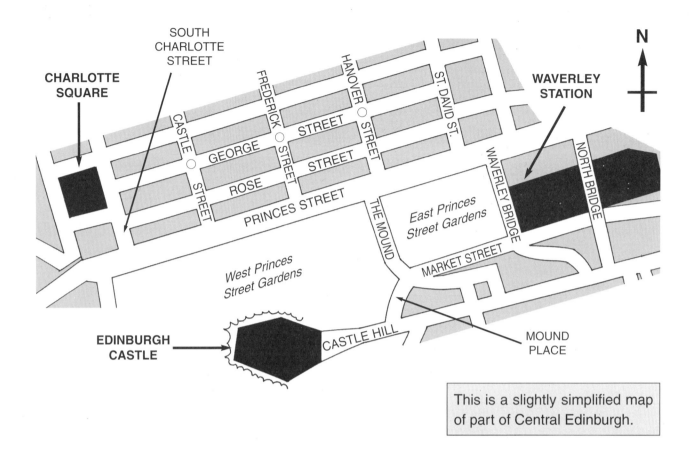

This is a slightly simplified map of part of Central Edinburgh.

Answer these questions

1. Which street leads to Edinburgh Castle ?

2. Is Waverley Station east or west of Charlotte Square ?

3. Is George Street north or south of the Castle ?

4. Which street runs over the top of Waverley Station ?

5. Which street separates West and East Princes Street Gardens ?

6. What does **St.** stand for in **St. David St.** ?

7. How would you direct someone from Waverley Station to the Castle ?

8. Can you direct someone from Charlotte Square to Waverley Station by 2 different routes ?

9. Which is the best known street in Edinburgh ?

Using fabric conditioner

To Use:

Comfort Regular fabric conditioner is ready to use. Simply use the no mess cap to dose straight into your washing machine drawer.

* Wash hands after use

* Do not pour directly on to fabrics

* Store between 5°C and 25°C

* Keep out of children's reach

* If splashed in eyes, rinse out well with water

 6-7 Kg 140 ml

For large loads or an extra dose of softness and freshness

 4-5 Kg 110 ml

For normal loads

 10 L 55 ml

For handwashing

A. Yes / No / Don't know

1. Is the fabric conditioner ready to use ?

2. Do you pour the conditioner straight on to the washing ?

3. Do you use the cap to measure the dose ?

4. Would you store the conditioner in the fridge ?

5. Should children use the conditioner ?

B. Answer these questions

1. How much conditioner does the cap hold ?

2. How much conditioner would you use for a normal load ?

3. How much conditioner would you use for extra softness ?

4. Would you use a 55 ml dose for woollens ?

5. Would you use the conditioner for all your washing ?

6. How many words can you make containing 2 or more letters, using letters from the word below ?

CONDITIONER

Warehouse storage instructions

All these signs appear on cardboard storage boxes in a supermarket warehouse:

KEEP COOL, DRY
AND AWAY FROM
DISINFECTANT, SOAP,
FRUIT, CHEESE ETC.

IMPORTANT
PRODUCT MUST BE
STORED AT -18°C / O°F
KEEP DEEP FROZEN

Store below 5°C, the temperature in the WELL of most retail dairy cabinets

GLASS

HANDLE WITH CARE

STORE THIS END UP

OPEN OTHER END

A. Which sign ?

1. Which sign is from a box full of ice cream ?

2. Which sign is from a box of margarine tubs ?

3. Which sign is from a box of packets of tea ?

4. Which sign is from a box of wine bottles ?

B. Make the words

Join the beginnings (1.) and endings (2.) to make words from the signs:

1.	fro	han	be	pro	re	o
2.	pen	tail	zen	dle	duct	low

C. Answer these questions

1. Should margarine be stored below freezing temperature ?

2. Why should tea be stored away from disinfectant or soap ?

3. Why should wine bottles be stored one way up but opened the other way up ?

4. Where is the 'WELL' of a dairy cabinet ?

Weather forecast

The Easter weekend will start off wet and cloudy. Heavy showers are expected in many areas tomorrow and on Saturday.

Sunday and Monday are expected to be drier with brighter spells, particularly in southern England and eastern Scotland.

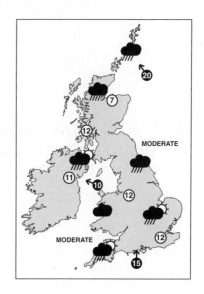

A. True / False / Maybe

1. Sunday will be better than Saturday.

2. All of the U.K. will be wet on Saturday.

3. 'Tomorrow' in the forecast is Friday.

4. The best weather on Monday will be in eastern Scotland.

5. There will be no weather in Wales.

B. Opposites

What is the opposite of these ?

wet   **heavy**   **brighter**   **start**   **many**

C. Which is the odd one out ?

1. tomorrow   Saturday   Sunday   Monday

2. wet   cloudy   spells   bright

3. Wales   Scotland   Northern Ireland   U.K.   England

4. eastern   Easter   southern   western   northern

D. Make up sentences

Make up sentences which contain these pairs of words:

1. Northern Ireland   sunshine

2. Scotland   wind

3. Wales   snow

4. England   showers

Form filling

Notes: • Please answer the questions in this booklet in ink, using CAPITAL LETTERS
• Please tick the boxes that apply

Mr ☐   Mrs ☐   Miss ☐   Ms ☐   Other ☐ →   *Please specify*

Surname/Family name _____

Other names (in full) _____

Address _____

_____

_____

Postcode _____ Telephone no. _____

National Insurance Number ☐ ☐ ☐ ☐ ☐

Date of birth ☐ ☐ ☐

Are you:

Single? ☐

Married? ☐

Separated? ☐

Widowed? ☐

Divorced? ☐

A. True / False / Maybe

1. You must write in capital letters.

2. All the boxes should be ticked.

3. 'Date of birth' should be given in words.

4. 'Surname' is the same as 'Family name'.

5. You can use a pencil to fill in the form.

6. You can use a biro to fill in the form.

7. A postcode contains both letters and numbers.

8. A National Insurance number contains both letters and numbers.

B. Fill in the form

Fill in the form for this person:

Miranda Anne Jones, 93 Bridgend Road, Birchgrove, Cardiff CF1 3ER
Tel. 029 2087 2777

1. Which boxes would you tick for her if she had been married but was now living with another partner ?

2. She was 28 on September 14th last year. Fill in the 'Date of birth' box.

3. What could be entered in these boxes ?

Other ☐ →   *Please specify*

Fire Extinguisher

BRITANNIA			
9 litre WATER			
GAS CARTRIDGE TYPE			
FIRE EXTINGUISHER			
TEST RATING 13A			
WOOD	LIQUID	GASEOUS	ELECTRICAL
✓	✗	✗	✗

TO OPERATE

1 REMOVE SAFETY PIN AND UNCLIP HOSE

2 DIRECT HOSE NOZZLE AT BASE OF FIRE

3 SQUEEZE HANDLE TO COMMENCE DISCHARGE. RELEASE TO INTERRUPT

RECHARGE AFTER COMPLETE OR PARTIAL USE

<u>WARNING</u>
DO NOT USE ON BURNING LIQUIDS OR LIVE ELECTRICAL EQUIPMENT

A. True / False / Maybe

1. The fire extinguisher sprays water on the fire.

2. The fire extinguisher sprays gas on the fire.

3. The fire extinguisher can be used on live electrical equipment.

4. The fire extinguisher can be used on burning plastic.

5. The fire extinguisher can be used on burning petrol.

6. The fire extinguisher can be used on burning gas.

7. The fire extinguisher won't start until the safety pin is removed.

8. The fire extinguisher jet can be stopped and started again.

B. Put these instructions in the right order

Squeeze handle to commence discharge.

Recharge after use.

Unclip hose.

Direct hose nozzle at base of fire.

Release handle to interrupt discharge.

Remove safety pin.

C. Word game

Make as many words as you can with 2 or more letters in them, using the letters in

EXTINGUISHER

Your Stars

GEMINI
22 MAY - 21 JUNE

Things are looking up this week for those born under Gemini. Your social life will pick up, especially at the weekend. It's a good time for romance, too. You'll be popular with others. Money-making opportunities look good - and you can afford to take the odd risk.

A. True / False / Maybe

1. Your social life will be good at the weekend.

2. You will have a new romance.

3. Everyone born under Gemini will be popular this week.

4. You could win the Pools this week.

5. This week will be better than last.

B. Sort out these jumbled words from 'Gemini'

coalis   mite   dewenek   rasts   file   yomen

C. Match the symbol with the sign

TAURUS	LIBRA	CANCER	SCORPIO	PISCES
a	b	c	d	e

Can you name the other signs of the Zodiac and give their dates ?

D. Yes / No / Sometimes

1. Do you always read your 'Stars' in magazines or newspapers ?

2. Do you believe everything that is said in your 'Stars' ?

3. Do you think that it is all a load of rubbish ?

4. Can you often think of events which agree with what is written ?

5. Do you think that the people who write the 'Stars' believe in them ?

A note on the table

Brian   4.30pm

You Mum rang. She's had a fall and hurt her arm. I'm going to take her to hospital. Can you go and get Emma from the Sports Centre at 6 o'clock? There's some pizzas in the freezer.

See you later — midnight?

Kate

A. True / False / Maybe

1. Kate rang Brian's Mum.

2. Brian's Mum has broken her arm.

3. Emma is at the Sports Centre.

4. Brian will be home by 5.30.

5. Kate will be home at midnight.

B. What do you think ?

1. Does Brian's Mum live on her own ?

2. Is Brian's Mum elderly ?

3. Do Brian and Kate live together ?

4. Are Brian and Kate married ?

5. What will happen if Brian is home late ?

6. Is Emma Brian and Kate's daughter ?

7. Does Kate usually make the tea ?

8. Does Kate drive a car ?

9. Are Brian and Kate both working ?

10. Why does Kate say *" - midnight ? "* ?

Easy chutney

MAKES 3 KILOS (6-7 LBS)

450g (1lb) stoneless dates
450g (1lb) sultanas
450g (1lb) apples
450g (1lb) onions
450g (1lb) dark brown sugar
575 ml (1 pint) vinegar
1 teaspoon salt
Ground black pepper
A dash of cayenne, allspice & ground ginger

Mince the dates, sultanas, apples and onions. Put them in a large bowl and stir in the sugar and vinegar. Add salt, pepper and spices. Leave to stand for 24 hours, giving the mixture a stir from time to time. Bottle in glass jars. This chutney is easy to make and will keep well.

from Rose Elliot's **Complete Vegetarian Cookery**

A. True / False / Maybe

1. The dates have to be chopped.

2. *450g* is the same as *1lb*.

3. A 'dash' is more than a teaspoon.

4. The mixture needs to be stirred all the time.

5. The chutney must be cooked for 2 hours.

6. White sugar could be used for the chutney.

B. What do you think ?

1. How many pieces of equipment will you need for making this chutney ?

2. Will the chutney be easy to make ?

3. Will the chutney be cheap to make ?

4. How long will it take to make the chutney ?

C. Opposites

All the words below appear in the recipe. Think of a word which means the opposite of each one.

large   **add**   **easy**   **dark**   **well**

Pub sign

The King's Arms
Relax in a real old tavern
REAL ALE
Food Served All Day
Midday - 10.00pm

✣ **Morning Coffees**
✣ **Afternoon Teas**
✣ **Dish of the Day** (12.00 - 3pm & 6pm - 9pm)
✣ **Lunch Served 12.00 - 3pm**
✣ **Dinner served 6pm - 8pm**

Guest Ale of the Month

60's music

A. Yes / No / Don't know

1. Is food served all day ?

2. Can you get food in the morning ?

3. Can you get *Dish of the Day* at any time in the day ?

4. Is dinner time 12 - 3 p.m. ?

5. Is The King's Arms open at 10.30 a.m. ?

B. Answer these questions

1. What is real ale ?

2. What is ale that isn't real ale ?

3. The King's Arms is said to be a 'real old tavern'. How old do you think it is ?
   50 years   100 years   200 years

4. What is a *Guest Ale of the Month* ?

5. The sign says *60's Music*. Will all the music be from the Sixties ?

C. Complete these

Cover up all the page above this and fill in the gaps below:

1. The King's _____

2. Guest Ale of the _____

3. Dish of the _____

4. _____ served all day

5. Afternoon _____

6. Morning _____

An inside job

A young woman went to visit a Young Offender Institution to give bible lessons. When she got back to her car she found that she had locked the keys inside it. She went back to see the Warden. He said that there were plenty of young lads inside who could get into her car. He went to ask which of the lads were in for doing cars. One of them said he was and he was taken out to the car. He picked up a brick and threw it through the windscreen !

from The Glasgow Herald

A. True / False / Maybe

1. The young woman gave driving lessons.

2. She had locked her bible in her car.

3. The Warden was a man.

4. All the young offenders were boys.

5. The Warden threw a brick through the windscreen.

B. Opposites

Find a word in the news item which means the opposite of each of these:

old	take	girls	opened
outside	lost	few	man

C. Sounds

1. **a.** How many words in the news item have a '**c**' sound in them (as in <u>c</u>old) ?

   b. How many different ways is the '**c**' sound spelt ?

2. *Find a word in the news item which has the same '**ou**' sound as each of these:*

round	tough	would	route

D. Same sound - different spelling

Think of a word which sounds the same as each of these words from the news item, but has a different spelling and meaning.

Example *(from the news item):* threw / through

to	see	there	which	for

Note from a Mail Order Company

Dear Customer,

Thank you for your order which has been sent under separate cover. The items listed below are out of stock and the refund shown is enclosed.

Code	Qty	Item	Price (inc.VAT)
H745	1	T-shirt, blue - Med.	8.99
R6381	1	Sweatshirt, red - XL	16.99
		Post & packing	*nil*
		REFUND	25.98

A. True / False / Maybe

1. All of the items are out of stock.

2. Red T-shirts are out of stock.

3. All red sweatshirts are out of stock.

4. The clothes are for a man.

5. Post and packing has been refunded.

6. The price included VAT.

7. The refund is in cash.

B. What do you think ?

1. What size was the T-shirt ?

2. What size was the sweatshirt ?

3. Why was there no refund of post and packing ?

4. Were the clothes good value for money ?

5. Is mail order a good way to buy clothes ?

C. Match the half sentences

The items are	your order.
The refund is	been sent separately.
The order has	out of stock.
Thank you for	enclosed.

The start of a romance

Joanne was going back to Devon because she had to. The thought of meeting Simon again had never crossed her mind !

Adam's eyes were warm with love as he kissed her goodbye through the car window.

"Have a good journey, darling," he said. "Sorry I haven't time to see you off from the platform."

They had driven to the station in silence. They both had things they wanted to say but they didn't say them. Silences, she thought, are often worse than arguments. At least you know where you are with an argument.......

based on a story from a women's magazine

A. Yes / No / Don't know

1. Does Joanne come from Devon ?

2. Is Adam going on the train with Joanne ?

3. Is Joanne in love with Adam ?

4. Is Simon an old friend of Joanne's ?

5. Do Adam and Joanne live together ?

6. Have Adam and Joanne had a lot of arguments ?

B. Tell someone else or write the answers

1. What does Adam look like ?

2. What does Simon look like ?

3. What do you think will happen in the story ?

4. Will the story have a happy ending ?

C. Word meanings

1. *Find words in the story which mean the opposite of each of these:*

   cold   bad   hate   hello   better

2. *Think of words which mean the same as these words from the story:*

   argument   silence   darling   journey   wanted

Get rid of mice

Pest-X Mouse Deterrent is a safe, easy-to-use, chemical-free way of getting rid of this common pest. When plugged into a standard electrical socket, it emits ultrasonic sound and an electromagnetic pulse. This is unpleasant to mice and drives them from the area. The unit is for indoor use only and will cover up to 230m² (2500 ft²). Also has a built-in night light.

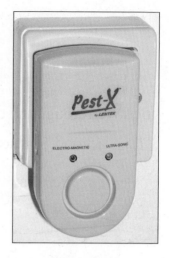

Please note: The sound does not affect cats, dogs, humans, fish or birds.

£39.95 *(plus post & packing **£1.99**)*

A. Answer these questions

1. Does **Pest-X** kill mice and rats ?

2. Is **Pest-X** safe for humans ?

3. Will **Pest-X** affect cats or dogs ?

4. Will **Pest-X** affect a pet hamster ?

5. Will the unit be noisy ?

6. Will 1 unit keep a whole house free of mice ?

7. Do you think there are any moving parts in it ?

8. Does the unit work off a battery or the mains ?

9. Do you think it is good value at £39.95 ?

10. Do you think it will work ?

B. What is wrong ?

Spot the error in each of these sentences

1. **Pest-X** will get rid of this common pet.

2. The sound is unpleasant to mince.

3. One unit will cover over 2,500 square feet.

4. Plug the unit into a standard electrical sock.

5. Also has a built-up night light.

6. The sound does not affect cats or bogs.

Advertisement for Pop Tour

from New Musical Express

A. Which is the odd one out ?

1. SHEFFIELD   HARROGATE   CARDIFF   BRADFORD

2. 0117   0191   0870   01702   0118

3. BRISTOL   READING   BOURNEMOUTH   BIRMINGHAM

4. Colston Hall   City Hall   Opera House   St. George's Hall

B. Two words into one

Join up these words to make the names of 6 places on the pop tour:

NEW   POOL   CHESTER   ON   MOUTH   MAN

SOUTH   PLY   CASTLE   END   BLACK   BRIGHT

C. Which place ?

Which place on the tour would be nearest to each of the places below ?

1. Durham
2. Swansea
3. Eastbourne
4. Colchester
5. Exeter
6. Stockport

Finding a playgroup

If you are looking for a playgroup, nursery or infant school:

- Go to see the playgroup or school. See a few if you have a choice. Talk to the people in charge, look at what's going on, ask questions.

- Trust your feelings. If you like the feel of a place, and the children seem happy and busy, that's a good sign.

- Talk to other parents whose children are at the group or school. Your health visitor may also be able to tell you about it.

- Talk about ways of getting your child to settle in at first.

based on part of Health Education booklet **Birth to Five**

A.   Agree / Disagree / Not sure / Other

1.   Playgroups are good for children.

2.   Playgroups are good for mothers.

3.   The people in charge always know what's best.

4.   The happiest playgroups are the most untidy.

5.   A playgroup is the same as a nursery.

B.   Find the right word

Without looking at the top of the page, choose the right word from the box to fill each of the gaps in the sentences below.

like	have	see	good
talk	look	hear	looking

1.   If you are _____ for a playgroup or infant school, go to _____ the playgroup or school.

2.   See a few if you _____ a choice.

3.   _____ at what's going on.

4.   If you _____ the feel of a place, that's a _____ sign.

5.   _____ to other parents at the group or school.

Yellow Pages

*These are some of the firms listed under **Drain & pipe cleaning** in the Carlisle and North Cumbria **Yellow Pages**:*

---

24 HOUR EMERGENCY CALL OUT

OIA AQUA JET

- Domestic & Commercial
- CCTV Surveys
- High Pressure drain &
- Pipe Cleaning
- Pipe Replacement & Repairs
- Cellar Pump-Outs

01228 522372
Mobile 07708 264608

Riverside House, Warwick Road, Carlisle

Alphajet Ltd,42 Fisher St...................Workington (01900)   607365

Andidrain,
Kingmoor Park Rockcliffe Estate,Carlisle..... Rockcliffe (01228)   672300
                                              Rockcliffe (01228)   672301
Andy Cannon Drain Clearance,
22 Etterby Lea Crescent,Stanwix......................Carlisle (01228)   595454
Aqua-Jet,Riverside House Warwick Rd,Carlisle,CA1.........07708   264608
Broughton Noel,1 Maitland St.......................Carlisle (01228)   522861
Dyno-Rod,
Brunstock Close,Louryhill,CA3..........................0800   112112
Santana Villa Crossfield Rd,Cleator Moor,CA25..................0800   112112

◼ J.R. THORNTON ◼

24 Hour Call Out

Drainage Specialist
Domestic And Commercial
High Pressure Drain Cleaning
Excavating & Repairs
COVERING WEST CUMBRIA

Tel : 01229 717289

Mobile : 07774143901
Lonning End Cottage Waberthwaite MILLOM

Jacques Cumbria Ltd,
Santana Villa Crossfield Rd...................Cleator Moor (01946)   813885

◼ MAYSON BROS LTD CONTRACTING ◼ SERVIVES

Drainage Specialists
CCTV Surveys
High Pressure Water Jetting

Tel: 01946 822308
www.mayson-bros.co.uk
Catgill Hall, Egremont

constructiononline

◼ NEWTONS PLUMBERS ◼

All Makes Of Elec. Toilets
Repairs & Service
Grunfoss-Edicare-Vortorpla
Tel: 01229 582 213
Mobile: 07803 079768
Newtonspulv@tiscali.co.uk
6 Priory Ct, Ulverston

SANIFLO REGISTERED ENGINEER

Answer these questions

1. Which firms are listed for these places ?
    - **a.** Carlisle
    - **b.** Workington
    - **c.** Cleator Moor

2. Is *Aqua-Jet* the same as *Alphajet* ?

3. Is *O1A Aqua Jet* in the box, the same as *Aqua-Jet* listed lower down ?

4. What do 'CCTV' and 'Bros' stand for in the *Mayson* advertisement ?

5. What is the dialling code for Egremont ?

6. How many of the firms look as if they could be 'one-man' businesses ?

7. Which firm repairs and services toilets ?

8. Which firms have the same address ?

9. How many times does the word **drain** appear on this page ?

10. In which advertisement is the word **services** incorrectly spelt ?

Brown and Brown / Reading Worksheets

Hospital appointment

OUT-PATIENT APPOINTMENT

An appointment has been made for you to be seen by:-

    MR. B. AHMED   or colleague

on:- THURSDAY THE 1ST OF APRIL

at:- 9.50 A.M.

When you arrive you should first report to the reception desk. Please bring any appointment cards you may have. If ambulance transport has been arranged for you please try to be ready from 8.30 am. for morning appointments and 12.30 pm. for afternoon appointments regardless of appointment time.

If it is impossible for you to attend it is important that you notify us as soon as possible so that another patient may have the opportunity to be seen. We will do our best to offer you a more convenient appointment.

On your first visit please bring a note of any tablets/medicine you may be taking.

NEW PATIENT

A. True / False / Maybe

1. The appointment is for the out-patient department.

2. You will be seen by Mr. D. Ahmed.

3. You do not need an appointment card.

4. The ambulance will arrive at 8.30 p.m.

5. You can change your appointment.

6. You should bring any tablets you are taking.

B. Word meanings

All the words below appear in the letter. Think of a word which means the same as each of them.

arranged   **notify**   **attend**   **opportunity**   **offer**

C. An out-patient's word puzzle

While you wait for your appointment, see how many words of 2 or more letters you can make from the letters in each of these words:

INFIRMARY   **APPOINTMENT**   **TABLETS**

Catherine Cookson

Catherine Cookson is known and loved by a large public through her vibrant and earthy novels set in and around the North-East of England, past and present. In **Our Kate** we see how it is that she knows her background and characters so well.

The 'Our Kate' of the title is not Catherine Cookson but her mother, around whom the autobiography revolves. **Our Kate** is a true story about living with hardship and poverty, seen through the eyes of the sensitive child and woman who won through to become Catherine Cookson, the warm and human writer we know today.

based on the cover blurb for **Our Kate** *by Catherine Cookson*

A. True / False / Maybe

1. The book is Catherine Cookson's life story.
2. 'Our Kate' is Catherine Cookson.
3. The author was born in North-East England.
4. Catherine Cookson writes novels.
5. Catherine Cookson was a sensitive child.
6. An autobiography is a true story.
7. 'Vibrant' means 'cruel'.

B. Answer these questions

1. What are novels ?
2. What is the difference between an autobiography and a biography ?
3. Where can you find the 'blurb' in a book ? What is it ?
4. What is fiction? Give the titles of 3 fiction books.
5. What is non fiction? Give the titles of 3 non fiction books.

C. Finish the pairs

Examples (from the passage): past and present; in and around

night and _____   now and _____

hot and _____   cut and _____

free and _____   high and _____

by and _____   give and _____

time and _____   here and _____

Housing Benefit form

What sort of building do you live in? *Place a cross X in a box*

Detached house ☐	Flat in a house ☐	Hotel ☐
Semi-detached house ☐	Flat in a block ☐	Board and lodgings ☐
Terraced house ☐	Flat over a shop ☐	Caravan, mobile home or houseboat ☐
Maisonette ☐	Bedsit or rooms ☐	Residential nursing home ☐
Bungalow ☐	Hostel ☐	
Other ☐		☐

Is there more than one floor? No ☐

Yes ☐ How many floors are there? ☐

Which floors do you live on? ☐

Do you and your household occupy only part of the building? No ☐

Yes ☐

A. True / False / Maybe

1. A 'hostel' is the same as a 'hotel'.

2. A bungalow is not a house.

3. A flat is different from a maisonette.

4. A bungalow can be semi-detached.

5. 3 or more houses joined together is a terrace.

B. Fill in the form

Fill in the form for yourself.

or

Fill in the form for a person who lives in a bedsit on the middle floor of a three-storey house.

C. Words from words

How many words with 2 or more letters in them can you make from the letters in each of these words?

1. MAISONETTE   2. RESIDENTIAL

NHS Organ Donor Register

Transplants are one of the miracles of modern medicine, but there are not enough organ donors. Every year, 400 people in the UK die while waiting for a vital organ transplant. One donor, after their death, can give life to several people and restore the sight of two more. A donor can give a heart, lungs, two kidneys, pancreas, liver, small bowel and corneas. More than 11.5 million people in the UK have already joined the NHS Organ Donor Register. To find out more, ring 0845 60 60 400.

from an NHS leaflet

A. Which is which ?

Match the parts of the body with the diagrams:

kidneys	heart	lungs	cornea	liver	pancreas
a	**b**	**c**	**d**	**e**	**f**

B. Yes / No / Maybe

1. Everyone should join the Organ Donor Register.

2. The eye can be used as a transplant.

3. The organs are removed before death.

4. A donor can only help one other person.

5. Eleven and a half thousand people are on the Register.

C. Jumbled words

The letters in each of these words can make a word from the extract above. *Sort them out.*

hated   **groan**   **slung**   **below**   **file**   **tow**

D. Beginnings and Endings (Prefixes and Suffixes)

1. *Think of 2 more words with the same beginning (prefix) as each of these:*

   transplants   **re**store   **al**ready

2. *Think of 2 more words with the same ending (suffix) as each of these:*

   don**or**   peop**le**   mill**ion**

Local News item

Handbag snatch foiled

A brave woman clung on to her handbag and forced her attacker to flee when she was stopped on Norcot Road, Reading, on Monday.

The 39-year-old was passing the dental surgery just before 6 pm when the teenager struck, running up to her and trying to snatch the bag from her shoulder.

She refused to let go and the would-be robber fled on foot towards the Dee Road estate.

Police are appealing for information regarding a youth aged about 17, who was wearing a black sweatshirt and red baseball cap.

*from the **Reading Chronicle***

A. True / False / Maybe

1. The woman had been to the dentist.

2. The attacker was 39 years old.

3. The attack happened on Monday afternoon.

4. The teenager wore a red baseball cap.

5. The teenager was from the Dee Road estate.

6. The teenager was a male.

B. Choose the right word

1. Her attacker was forced to _____ . (*flea / flee / flew*)

2. She refused _____ let go. (*two / too / to*)

3. He tried to snatch the bag _____ her shoulder. (*from / form / for*)

4. He was _____ a black sweatshirt. (*warning / wearing / worrying*)

5. The _____ - be robber fled on foot. (*wood / could / would*)

C. Finish these sentences in your own words

1. The woman was.....

2. The attack happened.....

3. The teenager should.....

4. The police will.....

5. Newspapers always.....

Wall Tile Spacers

To space tiles evenly

1. Snap off individual spacers.

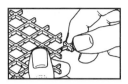

2. Fix first tile squarely in position and place a spacer at each corner. (Individual legs of spacers can be broken off to give T or L shapes for edges and corners.)

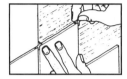

3. Fix next tile alongside, and place spacers at corners.

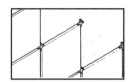

4. Continue until all tiles have been fixed.
Leave at least 24 hours for adhesive to set and then grout tile joints, leaving spacers in position.

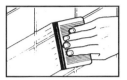

A. Put these instructions in the right order

Place a spacer at each corner.

Grout tile joints.

Fix next tile alongside.

Place a spacer at each corner.

Fix first tile squarely in position.

Snap off individual spacers.

Continue until all tiles have been fixed.

B. Find another word

*Replace the word in **bold italics** with another which means much the same.*

1. *Snap* off individual spacers.

2. Fix first tile squarely in *position*.

3. Individual *legs* of spacers can be broken off.

4. Fix *next* tile alongside.

5. Leave at least 24 hours for adhesive to *set*.

C. Answer these questions

1. Where would you use an L shape wall tile spacer ?

2. Will the spacers help to give a smooth, flat wall surface ?

3. Will the spacers show after the wall is finished ?

4. Will you need 4 spacers for every tile on the wall ?

5. Do you think it is easy to tile a wall ?

Tenpin bowling

 *Hollywood Bowl*

FABULOUS FUN FOR ALL THE FAMILY

HOORAY FOR HOLLYWOOD
A real fun packed family experience, 24 lanes with the very latest computer assisted scoring. It's fun ... it's entertaining ... it's ten pin bowling - Hollywood Bowl Style.

HOLLYWOOD DINER
For the hungry bowlers, check out our easy diner. A mouth watering menu that'll give you high energy for more of that Hollywood Bowling.

CUE 147
Take a break from Hollywood Bowling at Cue 147. Nine full size snooker tables for pot shots and professionals alike. It's easy on the pocket!

CANDY STRIKE
Pick & Mix sweets plus a range of pro equipment for bowlers of all ages.

BOWL BUDDIES
A sure way to score for children and beginners. Two inflatable tubes fill the gutters and keep the ball on course for the pins. A sure winner!

DI MAGGIO'S BAR
Say cheers in the atmosphere of Di Maggio's Bar. The perfect venue for a pre-bowl drink or to relax with friends after your game.

GIANT'S DEN PLAY AREA
Super safety zone for the under 5's who find that their bowling Mums and Dads get on top of their feet.

A. Numbers

Make a list of all the numbers *(words and figures)* in the advertisement.

B. Answer these questions

1. Where can you get something to eat ?

2. Is there an automatic scoring system for the bowls ?

3. Can you take young children along with you ?

4. What help is there for beginner bowlers ?

5. How many pins are there to aim at ?

6. Why is the snooker section called *Cue 147* ?

C. Headings

Look at the 7 headings in capital letters.

1. Which American words are used in the headings ?

2. What English word could be used for each American word ?

Scrabble inventor

The man who invented *Scrabble*, the world's most popular spelling game, died in April 1993 in New York at the age of 93. Alfred Butts invented *Scrabble* in 1931 but it was over 20 years before it really caught on. The owner of a New York department store got hooked on the game in 1952 and within a year it had become a national craze.

Alfred Butts was not very good at *Scrabble* himself because he was a poor speller ! He worked out the values of the letter tiles by counting the number of times each letter appeared on the front page of the *New York Times*. He made up sets of the game in his garage and sold them to local people. At first, the game was called *Criss-Cross*, then *Lexico* and it only became *Scrabble* in 1948. He made very little money out of his invention but he was quite well off, having spent his life as an architect.

A. True / False / Maybe

1. The inventor of *Scrabble* was called Alfred Butts.

2. Alfred Butts was born in 1900.

3. The game was invented in 1913.

4. Alfred Butts was a poor speller.

5. The game was first called *Lexico*.

6. *Scrabble* is the world's best-selling game.

B. How many endings ?

How many endings can you add to these words ?

1. invent

2. spell

3. call

4. depart

C. Longest word

What is the longest word you can make from these sets of letters ?

1.   S F M I E H L

2.   R L E L E S P

3.   S B U E E C A

4.   R P U L A P O

Benefit Form Declaration

Declaration

I understand that if I give information that is incorrect or incomplete, action may be taken against me.

I understand that I may lose benefit if I have

- not answered all the questions on this form that apply to me and my partner, if I have one, or
- not provided all the documents asked for.

I understand that the information I have provided may be checked with other sources. The information may be used for other purposes relating to the work of the Department of Social Security and the Employment Service and may be given to other bodies as permitted by law.

I declare that the information I have given is correct and complete.

I declare that if I have said that I want my Income Support, and any other benefits paid with it, paid into my account, I have read and understood the notes on this form about being paid in this way.

Please sign and date this form
This is my claim for Income Support

Signature

Date

/   /

Declaration from Income Support claim form

A.   True / False / Maybe

1.   The Declaration is part of an Income Support form.

2.   The Declaration is a legal statement.

3.   You must answer all the questions on the form.

4.   The information you give will be checked with other organisations.

5.   The information you give can be passed on to other people.

6.   If you give the wrong information, you could be taken to Court.

7.   You should sign and date the form.

8.   You can get someone else to sign the form.

B.   Choose the right beginning

Each of these words from the declaration begins either with **un** or with **in**. *Choose the right beginning for each word.*

___ come   ___ derstand   ___ formation

___ correct   ___ complete   ___ derstood

DVD / Video cover

RICHARD ATTENBOROUGH'S FILM

CHAPLIN

The cast of the film **Chaplin** reads like a *Who's Who* of screen talent. Richard Attenborough's much-praised film tells the story of the life and times of one of the cinema's most famous names - Charlie Chaplin.

It's a journey through the thrills and spills, the laughter and the sorrow that made up Chaplin's life behind and in front of the camera. The film follows his life through his early days of poverty in London; his first steps towards success in the music-hall; his beginnings as a film actor and then his days as director and star of some of the greatest films in the history of the cinema.

With Robert Downey Jr's dazzling performance as Chaplin, this is one film you don't want to miss.

based on the cover blurb of a DVD / Video

A. Yes / No / Don't know

1. Is the film called *Charlie Chaplin* ?

2. Is Richard Attenborough the director of the film ?

3. Was Charlie Chaplin born in London ?

4. Did Chaplin direct films as well as act in them ?

5. Was Chaplin a failure as a music-hall artist ?

6. Was Chaplin a comedy actor ?

B. Opposites

Give a word which means the opposite of each of these:

famous   poverty   success   beginnings   sorrow   miss

C. Finish these sentences

1. Richard Attenborough's film .....

2. Charlie Chaplin was .....

3. Chaplin's films are .....

4. In '*Robert Downey Jr*', **Jr** stands for .....

5. Films on DVD or Video are .....

Reduce the risk of cot death

Place your baby on the back to sleep from the very beginning. This will reduce the risk of cot death. Side sleeping is not as safe as sleeping on the back. Healthy babies placed on their backs are *not* more likely to choke.

At about five or six months old, it is normal for babies to roll over and they should not be prevented from doing so. This is the age at which the risk of cot death falls rapidly, but still put your baby on the back to sleep. If you find your baby on the front before five or six months old, gently turn your baby over but do not feel you should be checking for this constantly through the night.

It is good for your baby to play on the front when awake.

from Department of Health Leaflet

A. True / False / Maybe

1. The box on the right says '**ACK TO SLEEP**'.

2. Babies should be laid on their backs.

3. Babies will not choke if laid on their backs.

4. Babies can be laid on their sides.

5. Babies should never be laid on their front.

6. Cot deaths never happen when babies are laid on their backs.

B. Choose the spelling

Choose a spelling from the box to complete each of these words from the extract above:

_ _ ey	_ _ eir	_ _ oke
_ _ at	_ _ ich	_ _ ecking
_ _ is	_ _ ould	_ _ en

ch	**wh**
sh	**th**

C. Finish these sentences in your own words

1. If babies are laid on their sides, ...

2. When young babies roll over, you should ....

3. Cot Deaths happen more often when ....

4. The best way for babies to sleep is ....

Guest House advertisement

Bryn Bach Guest House, Minafon, BALA
North Wales LL23 7XY

★★★ Guest House   AA ♦♦♦

Rod and Sarah Williams welcome you to their luxurious guest house set in the magnificent countryside above Lake Bala. Four comfortable en suite bedrooms with television and tea-making facilities. Generous breakfasts, packed lunches and superb evening meals (pre-booked). Dogs by arrangement.

Open: March 1st - November 30th
B&B: *Double* pp £30-£35 *Single* pp £35-£40
2-night break: D, B&B pp £95 - £105
Tel./Fax: 01678 510998
Email: brynbachgh@supanet.com
Website: www.brynbachgh.supanet.com

N.B. This is not a real advertisement.

P6 🐕 🍴 🍷 💷 ☕ SP 🚫 ❀

A. True / False / Maybe

1. The Bryn Bach Guest House is in the town of Bala.

2. The Guest House has single rooms.

3. The bedrooms all have their own bathrooms.

4. Dogs can be accommodated in the Guest House.

5. The food is all home-made.

B. What's in the price ?

1. Are the prices per person or per room ?

2. Do the prices include packed lunches ?

3. How much does dinner cost on a 2-night break ?

4. How much more expensive is it for single B&B ?

5. Which times of year are likely to be the most expensive ?

C. Join up these half words

luxur	ities
arrange	erb
magnif	able
facil	ious
sup	icent
comfort	ment

Recipe from a Pasta packet

SPAGHETTI WITH A CREAMY PRAWN SAUCE

Serves: 4   Cooking time: 10 minutes

INGREDIENTS

400g (14 oz) Spaghetti
75g (3 oz) Unsalted butter
1 Small Leek or 2 Shallots, finely chopped
250g (9 oz) Cooked and Peeled Prawns
4 x 15 ml sp (4 tbsp) Dry White Wine
1 x 284 ml Pot Double Cream
1 x 15 ml sp (2 tbsp) Freshly Chopped Flat Leaf Parsley
Salt and Freshly Ground Black Pepper

METHOD

1. Cook the pasta according to pack instructions. Drain and return to
    the pan. Meanwhile, melt the butter in a frying pan and cook the
    leek or shallots for 3-4 minutes until soft. Stir in the prawns and
    cook for 2 minutes. Add the wine and boil rapidly for 2 minutes.
    Then add the cream, parsley and seasoning and heat gently for
    1 minute.

2. Pour the sauce over the cooked pasta and toss together well.
    Serve immediately.

Answer these questions

1. Where does pasta come from ?   *Spain / Italy / France / Germany*

2. Would this be a good recipe for slimmers ?

3. Could a vegetarian use the recipe ?

4. What items of equipment will be needed for cooking and serving the recipe ?

5. What does '**METHOD**' mean ?

6. How long do you think the pasta should be cooked ?

7. Do you think the cooking time given is correct ?

8. What time of year would be best for making this dish ?

9. Do you think the recipe is easy to make ?

10. Do you think this is a cheap recipe ?

Film 'firsts'

Films have now been around for well over 100 years. The first films were shown in the 1890s. It is thought that the first time that the public paid to see a film was in 1895 in the Grand Café in Paris. In the next year, 1896, the first film was shown in Britain at the Regent Street Polytechnic in London. The first Hollywood film was made in 1910, but all films were silent until 1927. Until that date, cinemas had a piano player who would play whilst keeping up with the action on the screen.

The first talking film was *The Jazz Singer* in which Al Jolson said the words "You ain't heard nothing yet!". Walt Disney first used stereo sound in 1940, but high quality sound for films did not come in until *Star Wars* in 1977. Nowadays, films are made for TV and DVD as well as for the cinema.

A. True / False / Maybe

1. The first film was made in 1890.

2. The Grand Café is in London.

3. Al Jolson was a singer.

4. All films were silent until 1927.

5. Walt Disney was the first person to use stereo sound.

6. *Star Wars* was made for TV.

'You must remember this...'
Bergman and Bogart
in *which film ?*

B. Which is the odd word out ?

1. keeping   talking   shown   nothing

2. player   actor   singer   writer

3. cinema   café   street   Polytechnic

4. London   Paris   Britain   Hollywood

5. screen   silent   video   stereo

C. Look through quickly

Answer these questions by looking quickly through the passage:

1. How many place names are there ?

2. How many dates are there ?

3. How many sentences are there ?

4. How many words begin with capital letters ?

5. Which sentence does **not** contain the words *film* or *films* ?

Jobcentre interview letter

Dear Mrs. Kaminski,

HELPING YOU BACK TO WORK

I am writing to ask you to attend an interview about your search for work and to make sure we are helping you as much as possible. Your interview is on:

Wednesday 5th November at 12.15 pm

If you fail to attend your interview and do not have a good reason, you could lose your Jobseeker's Allowance (JSA) and credits of National Insurance contributions. Please tell us immediately if you cannot attend your interview, for example because you have found work.

If you cannot show that you are doing enough to find work, a decision will have to be made on whether you are eligible for JSA and credits of National Insurance Contributions.

We will refund your travel costs (the cost of travel by the cheapest possible way) if your interview is not:

- on your normal day of attendance; or
- at your normal place of attendance and **you have to pay additional cost to attend**.

Yours sincerely,

Manager (on behalf of the Secretary of State)

(extract from a letter to a Jobseeker)

True / False / Maybe

1. The interview is on the first Friday in November.

2. The interview is in the morning.

3. Mrs. Kaminski has to see the Secretary of State.

4. She can cancel the interview at any time.

5. If she doesn't attend they could stop her benefits.

6. If she cannot prove that she is looking for work they will stop her benefits.

7. They will refund her travel costs.

8. She can choose the way she travels to the interview.

9. The Jobcentre staff are keen to help her find work.

10. The manager is a woman.

Worming a dog

Panacur Paste should be given orally by squeezing the paste from the syringe on to the back of the tongue after feeding.

Adult cats and dogs:

Give 2 syringe graduations per 1 kg bodyweight as a single dose.

Bodyweight	Single dose
Up to 1 kg	2 syringe graduations
1.1 to 2 kg	4 syringe graduations
2.1 to 3 kg	6 syringe graduations
3.1 to 4 kg	8 syringe graduations
4.1 to 5 kg	10 syringe graduations
5.1 to 6 kg	12 syringe graduations
6.1 to 7 kg	14 syringe graduations
7.1 to 8 kg	16 syringe graduations
8.1 to 9 kg	18 syringe graduations

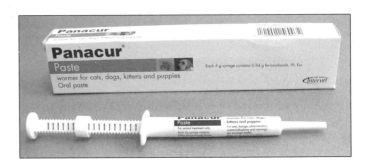

For example, to treat a 4 kg cat, twist the dose locking ring so that the bottom of it lines up with the 8th graduation. Depress the syringe plunger to deliver the correct dose.

A. True / False / Maybe

1. The paste is squeezed on to the back of the tongue.

2. The same paste can be used for cats and dogs.

3. The paste can be added to the animal's food.

4. The same paste can be used for kittens and puppies.

5. A full syringe holds 18 syringe graduations.

6. The syringe shown in the photo is set for 10 syringe graduations.

B. What is the correct dose ?

1. What is the correct dose for a 6 kg dog ?

2. What is the correct dose for a 2.5 kg cat ?

3. What is the correct dose for a 8.9 kg dog ?

4. What is the correct dose for a 1.9 kg cat ?

C. What do they mean ?

Explain what each of these words from the instructions means:

orally　　　　**graduations**　　　　**depress**　　　　**deliver**

HIV and AIDS

HIV is a virus that can damage the body's defence system so that it cannot fight off certain infections.

If someone with HIV goes on to get certain serious illnesses, this condition is called AIDS.

In the UK, there are three main ways in which HIV can be passed on:

- ❑ by having sex without a condom
- ❑ by a mother with HIV infecting her baby during pregnancy, birth or breastfeeding
- ❑ by drug users sharing needles, syringes or other equipment

There is almost no chance of getting HIV from treatment in the health service in the UK. It is completely safe to donate blood. You cannot get HIV from hugging, kissing, sharing baths or towels, swimming pools, toilet seats or from sharing cups, plates or cutlery.

At the moment, there is no cure for HIV or AIDS. There are cures and treatments for many of the illnesses that people with HIV are prone to. There are also drugs which reduce the level of HIV in the blood and delay the development of AIDS. Most people who take these drugs live longer and feel better, but there can be unpleasant side effects for some.

based on N.H.S. Health Education leaflets

A. True / False / Maybe

1. HIV is a virus.
2. You can get HIV from sharing drug needles.
3. You can get HIV from sharing someone else's cup.
4. You cannot get HIV from another person's blood.
5. You can get HIV from kissing.
6. You can get HIV from having sex using a condom.
7. You can get HIV from sharing someone's towel.
8. A mother with AIDS always passes it on to her baby.
9. There are drugs which cure HIV and AIDS.
10. HIV is a fatal disease.

B. Syllables

How many syllables are there in these words ?

Examples: **dam** + **age** *(2)*   **the** *(1)*   **ill** + **ness** + **es** *(3)*

that	other	passed	breastfeeding
completely	condition	infections	development
cannot	syringes	health	needles

Letter from the Bank

Dear Mr. & Mrs. MacDonald,

At the close of business on January 14th your current account was £135 overdrawn. Our records indicate that you have not applied for, nor have we formally agreed, an overdraft limit.

In accordance with our published charges for account services a fee of £20 has been debited to your account.

Whilst we appreciate that this may have happened as a result of an oversight, if you are experiencing any difficulties with respect to the operation of your account, please contact your local branch where someone will be pleased to talk to you.

Yours sincerely,

Mrs. M.K. O'Leary
Customer Services

A. True / False / Maybe

1. The MacDonalds' account is overdrawn.

2. The MacDonalds do not have an overdraft facility.

3. The bank wants to give them an overdraft facility.

4. The bank has charged them a fee of £2.

5. The bank would like to talk to the MacDonalds.

B. Words and phrases

Think of other words which could be used in the letter instead of these:

indicate   **appreciate**   **as a result of**

experiencing   **with respect to**   **operation**

C. Same word, different meaning

Put each of these words from the letter into a sentence which gives it a different meaning:

close   **current**   **charges**   **account**   **contact**

Instructions for a Microwave

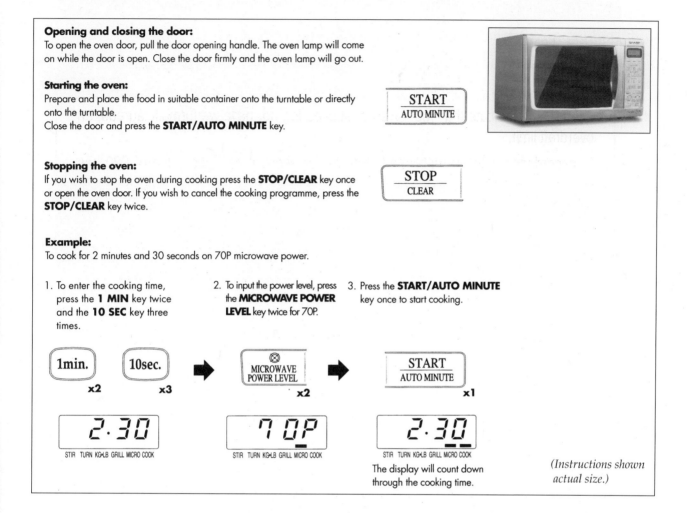

Opening and closing the door:
To open the oven door, pull the door opening handle. The oven lamp will come on while the door is open. Close the door firmly and the oven lamp will go out.

Starting the oven:
Prepare and place the food in suitable container onto the turntable or directly onto the turntable.
Close the door and press the **START/AUTO MINUTE** key.

Stopping the oven:
If you wish to stop the oven during cooking press the **STOP/CLEAR** key once or open the oven door. If you wish to cancel the cooking programme, press the **STOP/CLEAR** key twice.

Example:
To cook for 2 minutes and 30 seconds on 70P microwave power.

1. To enter the cooking time, press the **1 MIN** key twice and the **10 SEC** key three times.

2. To input the power level, press the **MICROWAVE POWER LEVEL** key twice for 70P.

3. Press the **START/AUTO MINUTE** key once to start cooking.

The display will count down through the cooking time.

(Instructions shown actual size.)

A. Yes / No / Don't know

1. Will the light go off when you open the door ?

2. Should you place food without a container on the turntable ?

3. Does the oven start automatically when you close the door ?

4. If you open the door during cooking, do you have to press the **START** button again to restart the oven ?

5. Do you have to press both the **1min** and the **10sec** buttons to set a time of 2 minutes and 30 seconds ?

B. What do you think ?

1. If you could only have one type of oven, which would you choose ?

    a. *a microwave oven*   b. *a gas oven*   c. *an electric oven*

2. What advantages, if any, are there in using a microwave oven ?

3. Are there any dangers in using a microwave oven ?

4. Does microwaved food taste different from food cooked in other ovens or pans ?

Index